READING

USING ANCIENT W
TO UNDERSTAND YOURSELF AND

G000242838

JOHN CREMER

 SUNMAKERS

Text ©2008-2011 John Cremer.

Diagram illustrations, cover design and layout by Ayd Instone.

Planetary type illustrations: Beham, (Hans) Sebald (1500-1550) from The Seven Planets

with the Signs of the Zodiac, 1539.

Published by Sunmakers, a division of Eldamar Ltd

157 Oxford Road, Cowley, Oxford, OX4 2ES, UK

Tel +44(0)1865 779944

www. sunmakers.co.uk

Version 1.1

The right of John Cremer to be identified as the author of this work has been
asserted by him in accordance with the Copyright, Designs and Patents Act, 1988.

No part of this publication may be reproduced, hosted or transmitted by any means
without the publisher's prior written permission.

ISBN: 978-0-9553917-2-9

www.readingpeople.biz

with thanks

To James Westly - friend, mentor and teacher of prescence.

The Maydays for the laughter and learning.

CONTENTS

INTRODUCTION

This book is an overview of a system of knowledge which has been hidden in plain view, right in front of us for our whole lives. We are driven to understand our fellow humans and are constantly baffled in the process.

Our enormous creative potential is continually squandered in destructive pursuits at both personal and global levels. Through a lack of self-knowledge we imagine ourselves to be simultaneously both greater and lesser than we truly are: greater, in that we believe that we act rationally from noble impulses and lesser, in our blindness to our true qualities. We claim the glitter of second-hand beliefs as having real value and so never seek the real gold within. We have truly "sold our inheritance for a mess of potage".

It is no wonder that we so often fail to understand other people. It is easier to ascribe to others the shortcomings that we deny within ourselves. Having labelled those we don't comprehend as "them" we then withhold from them the compassion and understanding that we ourselves desire.

Common to all faiths is the Golden Rule – to treat others as you wish to be treated; the elegant simplicity of this idea resonates in all sensible human beings.

The question is - How?

How do I treat people with respect when I don't understand why they do what they do?

How do I stop myself reacting in habitual ways?

How do I engage the finer qualities within myself with those of other people?

The purpose of this book is to offer an opportunity to access deeper levels of compassion and understanding for oneself and others.

Application of this system can allow one to both *know thyself* and
vive la différence!

By understanding the forces influencing human behaviour we can save much of the energy we waste in reacting to people's actions.

A Sufi tale –
You are in a boat on a river.
An empty boat floats downstream and bumps into your boat.
You carefully take this boat to the shore and tie it up safely so that the owner can find it and reclaim it.
Later, another boat, occupied, bumps into your boat.
You curse the occupier and call him names for his carelessness.

We will study the vehicle into which we are born. There are six basic models and we can discover quite easily which combination we have embodied to navigate through the world.

The type of vehicle we are operating profoundly influences how we experience our lives and other people. This is controversial information and can be seen as judgemental, pigeon-holing and not politically correct. With application, the knowledge becomes practical, liberating and life affirming. One is left with a sense of awe and wonder at the depth, power and potential benefits this system holds.

What you do with the knowledge is up to you. In verifying the concepts for yourself you invite their strength, poetry and mystery to bring harmony to your personal and professional relationships.

a bigger picture

"The unexamined life is not worth living" – Socrates

We are each, in many ways, the product of our culture, the time and circumstances of our life up to this moment. In Western Europe this is a largely materialistic and scientific based value system in which technology is venerated and any sense of connection to the unseen or unproven is seen as a quaint relic of our uninformed "primitive" past.

According to anthropologists, Homo sapiens has existed in the current form for around one hundred thousand years. For over ninety percent of this period, humanity lived in hunter-gatherer societies; spending about four hours per day to secure the basic essentials of life.

Having the same intellectual and emotional abilities as you or I they would inevitably seek to understand each other. These insights would be passed on through ritual, song, art and storytelling. Before the written word the knowledge would be refined, adapted and embellished as it was transmitted.

With the development of agriculture, people settled in larger communities and organised more complex institutions. As civilizations rose and fell the store of human knowledge continually evolved. Looking back we see definite peaks in the quality and expression of accumulated wisdom. We are baffled and possibly humbled by the achievements and motivations of the ancient Egyptians or builders of the Gothic cathedrals.

From our technologically advanced viewpoint it is tempting to see those that lived before us as somehow naïve or less informed. If we enquire more deeply it is discomforting to see that while we can instantly access vast quatities of information we yet find it difficult to discern the quality of this knowledge. We seem to know "the price of everything and the value of nothing".

There are great possibilities in recognising that ancient people used different symbols to express profound concepts which can deeply affect our lives in the present moment.

Universal truths are not affected by the passage of time; gravity acts exactly as it did in Babylon in 4000BC. A modern businessman desires an Aston Martin with exactly the same passion as a Roman senator desired the finest chariot. The external trappings change, human nature and objective truth remains the same.

In our era of globalisation and instant communication we need ancient wisdom more than ever. It is vital for us to understand ourselves and other cultures both quickly and at a deep level in order to interact effectively. Applying this knowledge at home, professionally and internationally promotes harmony and respect and enables each of us to make our unique contribution.

Western science studies phenomena through specialization; dismantling and separating the cosmos into ever smaller compartments. Ancient sages sought synthesis – finding connections in which elements of the cosmos reflected each other.

From a Western scientific perspective this approach is totally illogical, yet it is not easy to totally turn our backs on the accumulated wisdom of history; we sense something mysterious which seems just out of the grasp of our modern minds. It may helps to see this system as "alogical" i.e. outside of logic.

In the woodcut on page 6, produced by alchemists in the seventeenth century we see the planets personified as gods on Earth. This is one of many subtle references throughout history to a system of understanding that has long been "hidden in plain view".

Applying the System

It is vital to neither believe nor disbelieve this information; the value lies in the process of verification. Observe other people to see if they are recognisable as a type, find out what makes them tick; notice what draws or repels them and see how they react under pressure.

Always begin with the physical characteristics which are the strongest and clearest indicator.

It helps to find people who are obviously and strongly leaning towards one type.

Having clear examples of each type is like having a palette of pure colours; this makes it easy to see how they blend to create combined types. Start with the obvious ones and then refine the process; it is easier to do this with strangers or acquaintances than with those close to us.

Avoid the temptation to talk about this information as this can dissipate the focus needed to embody it in a lasting way. It also attracts a fair amount of scepticism and cynicism!

Observe how certain types are drawn to specific occupations; where a workplace is staffed mostly by one type it is easy to sense the energy of that type.

Applying the process to oneself is intriguing; imagine you are watching an interesting stranger. Observe without judgement; this is simply a way to see aspects of one's vehicle.

As a child I was fascinated by the Apollo mission and especially the buggy built to drive on the Moon. It had to meet very specific requirements, to function with less gravity and cope with the Moon's surface. Each of us has a vehicle we are operating on planet Earth and to know the vehicle means we can find ways to flourish in harmony with its capabilities. To judge and try to change the vehicle is pointless – the vehicle cannot change the vehicle any more than your car can change its own tyre! Simply allow the impressions to be received and one gains a sense of one's type. This changes the relationship between one's Self and the vehicle.

It is also useful to separate hardware from software.

Our type is the hardware that we inhabit and cannot be changed any more than we can change the colour of our eyes.

Our software is our life experience, culture, education and attitudes. This we can develop and evolve through training and the choices we make. We will always be expressing the software through the hardware. Our software can mitigate some of the limiting tendencies of our type and ideally complement and express the strengths. If we are in a situation or occupation which is fundamentally unsuited to our type then this awareness can be a powerful stimulus to make beneficial changes.

The Circle of Types

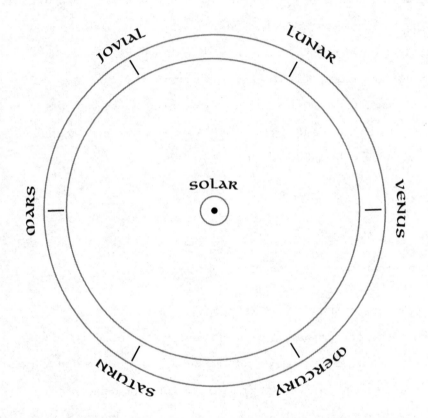

The circle traditionally represents the larger whole – literally "all encompassing". In this instance the circle represents the whole of humanity.

We plot six points on the circumference equidistant from each other. One way to visualize this is a clock face with a type at every other hour. On each point we place the visible planets of our solar system.

The Moon is placed at the first point, Venus at the second, Mercury at the third, Saturn at the fourth, Mars at the fifth and Jupiter at the sixth point.

We typically see people as a combination of two types e.g. Lunar–Venus, Venus-Mercury, Mercury-Saturn, Saturn-Mars, Mars-Jovial or Jovial-Lunar.

Occasionally, someone appears to be right on the point and they are considered to be a pure type e.g. Lunar, Venus, Mercury, Saturn, Mars or Jovial.

The Sun is at the centre and may add an additional influence to one's overall type.

This gives a framework to understanding the human experience; schematically the vehicle we are operating can be found represented at a point on this circle of planetary archetypes.

Using this structure it becomes possible with practice to calibrate exactly where one's type is found on the circle and explore how it relates to other types.

the hermetic principle

One of the oldest written records of esoteric knowledge is the *Emerald Tablet of Hermes Trismegistus* allegedly from the time of Ancient Egypt.

We find here the adage *As Above So Below* - the principle that the microcosm reflects the macrocosm. The atom is a model of the Solar System; the human lung structure reflects trees, leaf skeletons and river deltas and so on.

Here we seek to correlate mythology, astronomy, human anatomy and psychology. When previous civilizations looked at a night sky free from noise, light pollution and air pollution they were able to perceive the quality of *influence* of each planet. They saw this reflected in humanity and they left us clues to this vanished knowledge in the form of mythology. The Babylonians named the days of the week after the visible planets of the Solar System; in French and Spanish this remains unaltered. The Greeks and Romans connected the names of the planets with Gods and Goddesses and attributed psychological traits to them. Medieval alchemists produced drawings showing the temperaments and costumes of the planetary types and their typical occupations.

In the following chapters we will look at each type in turn using these guidelines:

The god or goddess

Each type is traditionally associated with a deity and a planet. We will explore their mythological and psychological attributes. There are remarkable parallels between the planets and their associated deities.

Polarity

Each type tends to be either negative or positive. There is no value judgement involved, neither is good or bad. Negative types tend to see the glass as being half empty, they automatically notice faults in others and potential drawbacks in situations. Positive types tend to see the glass as half full and automatically focus on upsides and possibilities.

Way of operating

Each type is seen as either active or passive. Active types act upon their environment and other people to fit their purposes. They are not content to leave things as they are and are often restless. An approximate modern term for active types is "Type A" personality. Passive types adjust themselves to fit their environment. They are often content to go along with the wishes of others and allow things to unfold in their own time. These are "Type B" personalities.

Physicality

One benefit of this system is that it each type has recognisable physical characteristics which have been observed for millennia and are unchanging. With practice one can assess the type of another person on first meeting them. There is a description of the traits and structure of the vehicle and how this affects our experience of life. Famous examples of each type add a visual dimension to the process.

Chief feature

The kingpin around which our perception of life revolves. This is simultaneously our greatest weakness and greatest strength; a double-edged sword which cuts both ways. Our vehicle is geared to react in certain habitual ways; once we see this we can use our chief feature for a purpose, it is a fine tool. When we are not aware, our feature is a primal energy force which may use us as a puppet for its own end. We may feel "right" and powerful when this happens but in reality we are acting unconsciously and possibly destructively.

Relationship to rules

Each type has a tendency to react automatically to authority and structure. A lack of awareness of this dynamic can cost us dearly in our professional and personal relationships without us ever taking responsibility for our part. Awareness of this reaction gives us the possibility to make different choices. We may never come to love the rules but we can avoid unnecessary suffering through tilting at windmills.

Behaviour at social event

Each type has a different response to social situations and varying levels of comfort in group interactions. To see this without judgement allows us to develop strategies to suit our type. We can determine where and when we are likely to flourish with others and avoid forcing ourselves into awkward scenarios.

Fruitful work environments

The arena in which the type will feel most able to manifest their qualities. So much of our time and creativity is taken up with our profession and we flourish in the right environment. To find "the right seat on the bus" can make a huge difference to our happiness in life and productivity at work. Conversely, to become aware that we are fundamentally unsuited to a certain role allows us to move on without trying to force ourselves to go against our nature. So let us now proceed to explore the six planetary types.

LUNAR

The Moon is sometimes seen as the child of the Earth. When the Earth was molten rock the Moon was torn off and cooled as our satellite. Remarkably the Moon is exactly the right size and distance from us that it precisely covers the Sun during an eclipse. The Moon and Earth orbit each other in such a way that one side of the moon is always hidden from the Earth – the dark side of the Moon. Precision and secrecy are attributes of the Lunar type. The Moon regulates the tides and has always been viewed as stirring up madness and obsession, a recent theory of this phenomenon is that before electric lights the full moon would keep people awake and sleep deprivation could tip vulnerable people over the edge. For a more poetic experience simply sit quietly outside under a full Moon – it feels odd!

The associated Goddess is Diana the huntress; jealous guardian of privacy and ruler of the night. She is typically depicted with hounds at her feet, a bow and arrows and a crescent moon in her hair.

The Romans called her Luna and the Greeks called her Selene.

This is the only negative, passive type.

Their attention is automatically drawn to details, especially what is missing or inaccurate and their response is often to withdraw or resist.

Lunar men are not often athletic; the hair is usually mousey and thin, their skin is pale or yellowish and the face round, with a weak or receding chin. There may be greyish bags or colouring under the eyes which are often small with a timidity to them. The chest is often small or even sunken, the shoulders rounded or sloped and there is little body hair. The voice tends to be thin and there is a slightly effeminate feel to them.

Lunar women have small breasts, not much of a waist and narrow hips, the hands and feet are small and delicate. They may well have a "china doll" appearance which makes them exquisitely beautiful and graceful. The hair is often thin and very straight and there can be a definite "moonish" look to their face with a chin that is weak or occasionally pointed. Again there is often very little body hair. Adult Lunars may look as if their bodies stopped developing part way through puberty.

This is an emotionally reserved type; their apparent coolness can leave them slightly removed from the general flow of social interaction. Lunars respect other people by giving them space and prefer the same consideration in return. As a passive type they are far more often intruded upon than intruding on others. As a negative type they are more aware of what they don't like than what they do, this holds for people too. For this reason Lunars make wonderfully true and loyal friends; once they have decided you pass muster they are constant and supportive especially in a crisis. They do not waste time and energy on emotional dramas so can be counted on when times are tough.

They are the "quiet heroes" in organisations and families, ever present in the background to offer guidance and support when appropriate. Lunars are the type most often misunderstood by the other types who judge them as being stand-offish, cold, secretive, serious, stubborn and dull. They do not like the spotlight on them and rarely seek attention from large groups of people. Still waters run deep, though. Lunars have a rich and intricate emotional life and care deeply about people and principles but are not demonstrative and consider it bad form to lose one's cool. Their attention to detail is supreme amongst the types to the point where it can look obsessive to outsiders. They value persistence, accuracy and detail and are the most meticulous people in their dress and work habits. They are able to live and work comfortably in a compact space. Disorganisation is quite disturbing to them and as children they were very likely to have enjoyed tidying their room and found security in routine.

Their inner focus can extend into a preoccupation with their digestion and they can be drawn to rather bland faddish diets which are "good for you" and involve simple ingredients. They often have a quirky sense of humour which relies on observing the foibles of others and their own sense of being misfits. The view from the Lunar section of the circle of types is one that sees others as loud, intrusive, careless, impatient, pushy, compulsive and clumsy. It is then no wonder that they prefer to spend time by themselves or their fellow Lunars! They see themselves as being clear-minded, consistent, persistent, reliable, patient and focussed.

China is a country which has a predominately Lunar population and outlook. We see this in the Great Wall, built to keep out strangers, their artwork which is highly meticulous and Chinese medicine with its thousands of acupuncture points, for example.

Recently China has sought a greater presence on the world stage and we can see the conflict of wishing to engage with other cultures while retaining privacy and control. It seems that, like the Moon itself, they are seeking to maintain the ideal orbiting distance.

Chief feature: Wilfulness

This is the awesome power of unshakeable determination; when Lunars decide upon a course of action they will not be swayed. Using the feature of Wilfulness, Lunars doggedly continue until they succeed in the endeavour, any obstacles only serve to strengthen the resolve and delays simply sharpen the focus. "Persistence Pays" is a Lunar motto as in the fable of the tortoise and the hare. When imposed upon they will resist, the greater the pressure, the greater the resistance. Many an active type has learned the futility of trying to budge a determined Lunar! They do not lose their cool in a crisis; the dramatic reactions of others produce deeper calm.

The downside of Wilfulness appears when a Lunar has taken a position and cannot be flexible. This is usually a refusal to participate and when threatened, bribed, reasoned with or persuaded they will dig in their heels and say "No". Once they are in this posture the feature has taken over and it is not possible for them to shift, it feels like life or death and it is important to respect their stance. It can be frustrating for other types to suddenly find a normally quiet

Lunar suddenly opposing them and refusing to budge. It is vital to recognise that the feature is in charge and to resist the desire to push harder, simply give them time and space.

China has a seat on the Security Council at the United Nations and always votes 'No' to any resolution that affects the internal affairs of another country.

Lunar and rules

Lunars stick to the rules to the letter and expect others to do the same; they flourish when the structure and guidelines are clear and will devote time and energy to fully establishing this before proceeding. An unhappy Lunar in an organisation will engineer a situation where they can take a fixed stand on a technicality in order to passively assert themselves. It can look like a chess move to an observer. This is a red flag to anyone involved in the situation and it needs to be addressed sensitively and privately.

Lunar socially

At a social event they will either be alone or talking with a fellow Lunar and criticising the food, music or other guests. They may be engaged in a supportive task that enables them to avoid excessive interaction. They will probably leave early after picking at the buffet. They do not enjoy the limelight, small talk or the unexpected – a surprise party in their honour is not a good idea!

Lunar at work

Lunars excel in careers where they can work on precise tasks with minimal interaction or supervision. They are happy working at night and in small spaces. They make superb accountants, librarians, bank clerks, research scientists, finance directors, computer programmers and proof readers.

Key words which will inspire their cooperation are: precise, long-term, clear-cut, defined, protocol, procedure department and reasonable.

Famous Lunars

Woody Allen, Pee Wee Herman, Mahatma Gandhi, The Mona Lisa, Damien Hirst, Olive Oyl, Heinrich Himmler, Christina Ricci, Bill Gates, Rowan Atkinson, Pete Doherty, Andy Warhol, Vladimir Putin, Helena Bonham-Carter, Gary Numan, Meg Tilley and Data from *Star Trek*.

Lunar Animals

Mice, donkeys, moles and tortoises are Lunar animals, as is Eeyore from *Winnie the Pooh*.

♀

VENUS

The planet Venus is seen as the sister of Earth as it is of similar size and gravity. Venus appears in the night sky as the morning star and evening star, second in brilliance to the moon. It has always been described as beautiful and sensual and many ancient sacred sites monitored the movements of Venus. It takes 243 days to rotate on its axis, making a day on Venus eight months long. Although Venus is the closest planet to Earth it is very hard to observe as it is covered in clouds.

Venus is the goddess of love and sensuality and is associated with nature, abundance, nurturing and raising children. There are numerous classical sculptures and depictions of Venus as a voluptuous woman often with children in a natural setting.

This is a positive passive type.

Their attention is drawn to more active types and their tendency is to live through others and to go along with the status quo.

Physically Venus women tend to be soft and fleshy, the skin is smooth and sensuous, the hair is dark and thick often with a lot of body hair, the lips are plump and full, breasts large and the hips may be very wide. They are the classic "Earth Mother" type. Their voices can be soothing and melodious.

Venus men are large all over with a lot of dark body hair and soft features. They often carry weight in their legs and thighs and have a grounded feeling. Venus men keep their hair into old age and it stays dark with little greying. They may be very large yet have a soft gentle voice.

These are the slowest moving of all types and very easy going, they will drop whatever they are doing (which may not be much!) to be there for someone else. Their positive polarity shows up in unconditional acceptance of others, they are prone to see the best in people. In the eyes of a Venus most people are basically good inside and will act decently if treated well.

As the Goddess of love they seem to feel that love cures all and are willing to take care of those that most people give up on. Their passivity is seen in a willingness to let others set the agenda; they have more of a sense of "we" than "I". They are oriented to family, tribe or team and can almost go into a state of suspended animation when not connected to one of these.

They do not like to stand out from the crowd and may hide their talents in order to fit in. It is easy to forget their name or overlook them.
It can be difficult for a Venus to know who they are and what they want. Serious self-enquiry can be challenging for a Venus as it is usually a sense of discontent which prompts us to look within.

Venus types avoid discontent by adjusting their expectations and requirements downwards. It can come as a shock to a Venus type to wake up and realise that they have spent a decade doing very little. Other types – especially active ones tend to judge Venuses as lazy, adrift, co-dependant, unmotivated, vague and a soft touch. If they acquire a taste for cannabis, which many Venuses do, it can lead to a lifetime "vegging out" in a haze of inaction and stupor. They will tend to see others as hyper, selfish, pushy and ungrateful while seeing themselves as kind, peaceful, easy-going and friendly. They go with the flow and like things comfortable and people find it easy to relax around them. To spend time with a Venus friend is very refreshing as you don't have to do much. They radiate a healing, calming influence and may have a circle of friends who can't stand each other, while they get along with all of them. This type comes closest to embodying unconditional love, simply accepting others as they are without an agenda for growth and improvement.

When hugging a Venus type one feels time stand still and one has a sense of sinking into a safe, warm place. Venus women, in particular, have the ability to absorb stress and sickness from children. A crying baby will often become silent when swept into the soothing Venus embrace.

Venus nations

Hawaii and Polynesia are Venus countries; historically Venus types lived where life was easy and simple, places that are viewed as Paradise. On arrival at Honolulu airport one receives a garland of flowers around the neck and a kiss on the cheek. This does not happen at Heathrow! Any culture that has a "mañana" attitude and enjoys a siesta has a strong Venus element.

Chief feature: Non-Existence

This is an ability to totally put one's self aside without an agenda. The quality of this feature lies in being able to be there 100% for a cause or another person, true service. They can be a very powerful "power behind the throne".

By not asking for much they can become highly valued to an organisation and be the cohesive force which holds teams or families together through turmoil and also nurtures talent. The downside of Non-Existence appears when decisions need to be made and action taken; it can feel as if there is literally no one in there, the body is present but the personality is absent. A Venus may not "show up" for their whole life. They may be chronically late. They can grow to resent those that assert themselves and sink into self pity and sabotage. Under extreme prolonged duress they may snap and explode becoming uncontrollably angry, "going postal" is the term.

Venus and rules

They have a laissez-faire attitude to the rules, generally going along with them. If someone else breaks the rules they are usually not bothered enough to take action to enforce them and would rather overlook infractions than rock the boat. This is why reporting a crime in Mexico can be a highly comedic experience.

Venus socially

At a social event Venuses will be serving food, listening to sob stories, giving back rubs or taking care of the kids. They may not even show up at all.

Venus at work

They flourish in occupations such as counselling, massage, social work, nursing, gardening, child care and supportive roles to strong individuals or organisations. They respond to keywords such as: team, we, us, team-player, co-operate and help.

Famous Venuses

Marlon Brando, Pavarotti, Liv Tyler, Forest Whitaker, Droopy, The Venus de Milo, Nigella Lawson (the domestic goddess!), Jennifer Lopez, Ernest Borgnine, Demis Roussos and Debussy - whose lush music reflects his sensual nature.

Venusian animals

Sloths, slugs, chocolate Labradors, bloodhounds and cows are Venus animals.

☿

MERCURY

Mercury is the innermost planet of the Solar system and also the smallest. It is difficult to observe from Earth due to its eccentric orbit and proximity to the Sun. Mercury is only visible at twilight and is "full" when it is behind the Sun.

Mercury is the winged messenger; God of commerce, thieves, profit and communication. He was known to the Greeks as Hermes and carried the caduceus.

This is a negative active type.

Their attention is drawn to the effect they have on other people and their tendency is to influence others using words and imagery.

Mercury men are wiry in stature, medium height, the hair is dark and often curly, eyes are brown and bright, hips narrow, hands small and well manicured. Their teeth are often white and even. They may well sport a small black moustache. They tend to dress well and appear dapper.

Mercury women are fairly short with trim figures, smallish breasts and narrow hips and waist, dark flashing eyes and the teeth are white, small and even. The voice is often strong. The smile may well be dazzling and consciously used to good effect.

Both genders tend to look younger than they are and this gap between real and apparent age widens as they grow older, with or without cosmetic surgery.

This is the fastest moving type, physically and mentally, filled with restless nervous energy. Mercurys are almost incapable of going from A to B, they don't want to miss anything so will deviate from a straight path. They are concerned with how they appear, often "power dressing" in red, black and white.

Mercurys do not enjoy being in situations that they do not control and will often pay careful attention to the person in charge of a situation. They can be very seductive and persuasive, having a way with words and an instinct for what others want to hear. This leads them to having chameleon-like abilities to adapt their persona to fit any situation. Outfit, tone of voice and subject matter can change in an instant.

Mercurys thrive on attention and love being onstage while at the same time feeling insecure, needing reassurance and not wanting to show this need. Other types may find it difficult to trust them and judge them as being slick, evasive, insincere, scheming and pushy. If they acquire a taste for cocaine, which some do, it exaggerates their sense of distrust and paranoia and makes them intolerably hyper to be around.

The metal quicksilver is named after Mercury and is the only metal that is liquid at room temperature; it also slips through one's fingers. Authentic self enquiry can be difficult for a Mercury who has invested time and energy in their persona. Caught between the desire to impress and the awareness that they are projecting an image, they can be prone to distrust and find it hard to drop their guard. They see themselves as creative, dazzling, confident, highly motivated and inspiring. They may well have these talents in abundance and can easily enthral an audience.

Mercurys have the ability to find connections that others miss and direct people towards potential opportunities. They are superb networkers, communicators and idea generators but may lack the patience to complete projects; preferring to turn the implementation over to more passive types.

They often feel frustration with other types; seeing them as slow, literal, unimaginative, docile and pushovers. Mercurys will never be famed for their patience! Their wit and sparkle is infectious and they have a tremendous ability to bounce back from difficulty; they do not take "No" for an answer. There is something of the spoilt grandchild about a Mercury but their abundant charm leads us to make allowances for them.

Chief feature: Power

This is the ability to get other people to do what they want, using words. The quality of Power lies in inspiring others by opening them to new possibilities. Mercurys like to be close to the action and generate passion and excitement for new projects. As a weakness; Power shows up as manipulation, insincerity and a determination to save face at all costs. Mercurys in the grip of this feature can lose track of the line between their honest truth and the habit of telling people what they want to hear; this can tip into deep suspicion. Al Pacino in the film "Scarface" played this feature to perfection. Machiavelli is a classical depiction, as is the character Iago in "Othello".

Mercury and rules ·

Their relationship to the rules is to bend them, as the rules are seen as applying only to people slower or less creative than them. This can develop into fraudulent behaviour e.g. where tax avoidance becomes tax evasion. Mercurial creativity and their desire to sail close to the wind can lead them into some grey areas. On the other hand their intolerance of red tape can promote highly effective problem solving.

Mercury socially

At a social event the Mercury is centre stage and the party begins when they arrive, fashionably late, networking, joking, flirting, constantly on the move, wheeling and dealing. Ideal jobs include: sales, advertising, lawyers, entertainers, actors, spin doctors and DJs.

Famous Mercurys

Charlie Chaplin, Amy Winehouse, Marcel Marceau, Bugs Bunny, Victoria Beckham, Jack Nicholson, Eddie Murphy, Diana Ross, Freddie Mercury, Naomi Campbell, Colin Farrell, Joan Rivers, Tony Robbins, Adolph Hitler and Mother Teresa.

Mercury animals

Chihuahuas, hyenas, parrots, magpies, mackerel, Jack Russells and foxes are Mercury animals; as are the cartoon characters Speedy Gonzalez and the Road Runner.

SATURN

Saturn is the sixth planet from the Sun and the second largest. The rings are the most obviously striking element of Saturn, composed mostly of ice with some rocks and dust. Saturn has sixty known moons.

Saturn is the God of agriculture, justice and strength and is also linked to Kronos (Time) and is depicted as the Grim Reaper with his scythe. He is associated in mythology with teaching, rules and limitation.

This is a positive active type.

Their attention is drawn to people's potential and their response is to direct and organise.

Saturn women tend to be tall, bony and athletic; the face is long, hair blonde, eyes are blue and they may have a masculine or androgynous feel. This type is currently idealised as fashion models. They tend to move in a graceful and deliberate manner.

Saturn men are tall and long limbed; the face can be narrow and craggy with a prominent nose and chin. The hair is usually fair and the eyes are often blue and piercing. They move slowly and hold themselves in a commanding manner and may appear dry and aloof.

Saturns feel tall, they have an overview of other people's affairs and exude a natural sense of authority; people literally look up to them. They have a strong affinity with justice and feel the world would be a better place if only everyone were more like them; they can give off an air of being slightly disappointed that they are not.

Saturns tend to be ascetic; they may see their journey through the world as a long march down a narrow, straight path. There is usually a lofty goal at the end and they expect to make personal sacrifices along the way. This is done for a higher cause and Saturns expect the same sacrifices of others. They believe they know what is best for other people and display a strongly altruistic nature. They may have difficulty loosening up and having a good time, preferring purposeful activity or conversation to a party and small talk. Their home environment is uncluttered to the point of austerity and they have an active distaste for knick-knacks and cheap souvenirs.

Saturns radiate a paternal feeling of safety in their presence, they like to take lost souls under their wing and offer them guidance. They are always immensely proud of the achievements of their protégées. They have a strong antipathy towards injustice of any kind and are often drawn to organisations which promote fair play. Saturns see themselves as capable, trustworthy aesthetic, sober, prudent and balanced. They see most other types as undisciplined, compulsive, self-indulgent, short-sighted and naïve. They are prone to deliberate before acting and may miss a moment of opportunity because they are carefully weighing up the pros and cons. Other types see them as grey, dithering, stingy, judgemental and puritanical.

Saturn nations

Parts of Scandinavia are populated almost exclusively by Saturns and we see this in their social welfare systems which are highly paternal. Holland and Switzerland are Saturn countries and the British Empire was a mostly Saturn institution. Saturns have a natural affinity for philosophy, especially of a dry, theoretical nature and are able to apply their overview to complex scenarios.

Chief feature: Dominance

This is taking charge and delegating in a logical, organised manner.

As a quality they bring a benign paternal influence to those they mentor, clearly leading organisations and individuals to a better way of life. With patience and wisdom they offer guidance and never ask more of others than they do of themselves. One is inspired to higher standards with a Saturn at the helm. When Dominance takes over, a Saturn becomes repressive, isolated, dogmatic, grey and constipated. The classic depiction of a miser is a Saturn ruled by Dominance and controlling his desires and people around him. They can sink into a very bleak and judgemental world. This is the typical picture of melancholy.

Saturn and rules

When it comes to the rules, Saturns make the rules because they know what is right, fair and best for everyone. They can see the big picture and make far reaching decisions.

Saturn socially

At a social event you will find Saturns sipping fine wine in a group and philosophising or giving paternal advice to a hapless passive type.

A deliberating group of Saturns feels like a clump of beech trees.

Saturn at work

Saturns make good teachers, judges, coaches, consultants, directors of companies, scientists, philosophers and organisers.

Famous Saturns

Charlton Heston, Katherine Hepburn, Prince Phillip, Uncle Sam, Gwyneth Paltrow, Abraham Lincoln, Carly Simon, Keira Knightley, Vanessa Redgrave, Sven Goran Ericsson, Maggie Smith, General Kitchener and Elle Macpherson.

Saturn animals

Great Danes, storks, herons, stick insects and giraffes are Saturn animals.

MARS

Mars is the fourth planet from the Sun and is known as the red planet due to it being largely covered in iron oxide dust. The biggest storms in the Solar System erupt periodically on Mars and darken the surface for months.

Mars is the God of war.

This is a negative active type.

Their attention is drawn to challenges and their approach is to meet them head-on.

Mars men are short with a bullet shaped head, thick neck, small mouth ears and eyes, short, thick fingers, barrel chest and bandy legs. Their hands often hang with the palms facing backwards, the hair is red and skin is pale with freckles.

Mars women are short, tomboyish and resilient. The face is often squareish with blue eyes and a small mouth. Their shoulders are square, breasts small and the demeanour slightly masculine.

It appears that the majority of Lesbian women are Mars types.

This type is built for action, going straight from A to B in a hurry; they are not patient. Obstacles are to be removed or flattened, the idea of altering one's course is seen as weakness. Mars are refreshingly blunt and direct in speech and action. They are prone to suffer from "mechanical honesty"- telling the bald truth when it may be better to be diplomatic - and have a strong intolerance of injustice. Mars children are the ones that will go bright red in the face and shout "It's not fair!" loudest and longest of all types. Adult Mars like to unwind by drinking and being loud; a holiday for a Mars is like a military campaign with targets, dates and strategy; extreme sports and high risk activities are their idea of relaxation. They have a high capacity for enduring pain, relishing the charge they get from testing their strength against the world and are quite proud of any suffering they have survived.
Their systems are filled with adrenaline, causing the continual need to move and express; they are highly sexually charged and can become unpleasant if they do not have sex frequently.

Other types judge Mars as hot-headed, tactless, bull in a china shop and crude; most Mars would agree and not care! They see themselves as strong, brave, hard-working, hands-on, salt of the earth people. Their humour is earthy and bawdy; they will respect anyone who confronts them toe to toe, even if they totally disagree with everything they stand for. They like a nice, straight clean fight and don't mind losing a fair fight. Once a Mars has got the measure of someone they make a steadfast and loyal friend willing to go the distance when called upon. The stirring speech "Once more into the breech dear friends.... " from Henry V is poetry to the ears of a Mars.

Others types are viewed by Mars as being lazy, soft, prissy, slow, airy-fairy and over sensitive.

They see things in black and white and have no time for nuances or shades of grey. Mars value self reliance and have little interest in half-measures or small print. They have an affinity for protecting the underdog and are drawn to fighting for causes, especially those connected to righting perceived injustices. Mars tend to be on the front line at demonstrations and revolutions and are found in abundance in the military. Having a target focuses their energy and frees them to act forcefully without doubt or questions. In personal development work Mars exercise ruthless self-enquiry and are very willing to give unsolicited direct feedback to others.

Chief feature: Destruction

This is a compulsion to move forcefully against obstacles or adversity.

As a quality this fuels a willingness to go all the way; total honesty and determination to discover the truth in all situations. Alexander the Great cutting the Gordian knot captures this spirit of fierce courage and clarity. When gripped by destruction Mars can be totally reckless and out of control, destroying marriages, careers and friendships for no purpose beyond the adrenal thrill of the moment.

A Mars CEO can be more focussed on destroying the competition than on succeeding. When turned inwards this feature becomes self-destructive through drugs, alcohol, affairs, over-eating, reckless driving or other high-risk behaviour.

Mars and rules

Mars' relationship to the rules is that of law enforcer, using violence if necessary; dividing the world into good guys and bad guys, they are always ready to take down the bad guys.

They are the immune system of a country or organisation, keeping out dangerous intruders.

If the system they are defending becomes corrupt or unfair Mars will be the first to rebel.

Mars socially

At a social event they will be drinking, loudly cracking crude jokes and comparing battle scars and war stories. If there is a barbeque on a balcony it will be surrounded by Mars drawn to the twin attractions of burning fat and the possibility of falling off.

Mars at work

Mars thrive in construction, demolition, security, police work, the armed forces, sports coaching and debt collection. They can excel in sales if given clear targets to meet and make superb operations managers. Words that inspire a Mars in the workplace include: challenge, struggle, bullseye, front-line, shake-up, push through, campaign and crisis.

Famous Mars

James Cagney, Chuck Norris, Mike Tyson, Geri Halliwell, Klingons, Billie Jean King, Vincent Van Gogh, Juliet Stevenson, Wayne Rooney, Ellen MacAthur, Alexander the Great – who simply bisected the Gordian knot with his sword rather than untie it, John F. Kennedy and Kenneth Branagh.

Popeye is plainly a Mars - "I am what I am! "

Most celebrity chefs are Mars – lots of heat, stress, danger and shouting of obscenities!

Mars animals

Tasmanian devils, piranhas, sea bass, lions and bulldogs and Yosemite Sam.

♃
JOVIAL

The planet Jupiter is fifth from the Sun and is the largest planet in the Solar System with the strongest magnetic field. Uniquely, Jupiter radiates its own heat; more than it receives from the Sun. Jupiter has at least 63 moons, one of which is bigger than the planet Mercury.

Jupiter is king of the Gods and the God of the sky and thunder. The Greeks called him Zeus.

This is a positive, passive type.

Attention is drawn to the arts and creativity and their response is to determine and maintain their role in the terrestrial drama.

Jovial women tend to be large and round with a fleshy face, large breasts, deep chests, full waist, narrow hips, and thin legs; their voice and laugh is often rich and booming. The men carry most of their weight on the chest and upper body, sometimes with spindly legs, the face is full, even jowly; they tend to lose their hair and can look older than they really are.

Jovials have a regal, grandparental feel; they love to have people around them in a jolly, harmonious environment. They instinctively cast themselves in leading roles in social and personal situations. Just as the planet Jupiter

radiates heat, so Jovials radiate personal warmth to their large circle of friends. They love to coach, guide and mentor and see the success of their protégées as a reflection of their own qualities. Jovials are lively raconteurs and most of their stories are about themselves. They enjoy spending money and are not good at budgeting, believing that they should simply buy what they want regardless of their bank balance. They see other types as narrow, unimaginative, tight-fisted, pedantic riff-raff. George IV was a classic Jovial who bankrupted the treasury to build the Royal Pavilion in Brighton. Chinese and Indian art were in vogue so he blended both.

Jovials do not believe that "less is more" they enjoy the arts and the finer things in life; their environments can be cluttered with the accoutrements of their eclectic pursuits. They see themselves as cultured, gifted, dignified, gallant, courteous, interesting and natural leaders. Disharmony is painful to them and they feel upset if their friends suffer or argue. They will often work behind the scenes to mend rifts and can make ideal diplomats. Jovials are unthinkingly generous to their friends while unconsciously keeping track of the gifts they have given. They can then become demanding when they want something and the balance sheet comes into sharp focus.

Other types judge Jovials as being pompous, self indulgent, arrogant, touchy drama queens. They have a way of making people feel privileged to be asked to do something for them, as if they have been specially chosen for the task. Mockery and ridicule are not easily forgiven and they can hold a grudge for years if their pride is wounded.

They are happiest when celebrating success with friends and admirers; toasting, joking and making the walls reverberate with raucous laughter. Their worst experience is during times of financial constraint and a loss of social prestige. They will sometimes maintain an image of abundant success with some highly creative use of credit cards and loans. To incur the wrath of a Jovial results in banishment from their Royal court; to be thrust into the outer darkness and wither far from the radiance of the Jovial aura is the worst punishment they can imagine. Jovials are found in Eastern Europe, especially Poland and unlike most types they are quite willing to listen to the polka.

Chief feature: Vanity

This is the innate belief that they are uniquely special, capable and accomplished. As an asset this gives Jovials the confidence to explore new vistas and share the treasures of their experience with their retinue.
Pure Jovial Vanity has an endearing and infectious quality. Excessive Vanity brings arrogant self delusion about the degree of their abilities, a weakness for boasting and a craving for flattery. They can become manipulative and surround themselves with "yes men" and be spiteful to those who are less than totally fawning. They become the archetypal tyrant king or queen or a dictator.

Jovials and rules

Jovials appreciate rules that promote harmony, decorum and the circulation of abundant wealth. They find deep offence with any restrictions upon their spending and see these sorts of petty rules as only applying to the "little people".

Jovials socially

At a social event they will be hosting and orchestrating, holding court loudly and often drinking and eating to excess. They love big parties and like to make grand, sweeping entrances and exits; ideally with a large entourage. Jovials will often make it their mission to single out a social misfit, cheer them up and bring them into the swing of things – involuntarily if necessary!

Jovials at work

Jovials excel in the arts, making great orchestra conductors, classical musicians, publicans, linguists, diplomats, restaurant hosts, teachers and chefs.

Famous Jovials

Santa Claus – he knows who has been good! Rembrandt, Falstaff, Aretha Franklin, Shelley Winters, Chris Farley, Oprah Winfrey, Tommy Cooper, Dawn French, Richard Griffiths and Winnie the Pooh.

Prague is a Jovial city.

Jovial animals

Whales, elephants, pigs and walruses are Jovial animals.

Toad of Toad Hall is a classic Jovial – "But I must have it, I simply must! "

COMBINED TYPES

Only rarely do we encounter someone who can be considered to be a pure type. We are all combinations of two types in varying degrees on the continuum Lunar-Venus-Mercury-Saturn-Mars-Jovial-Lunar. It is possible to be a Mars-Jovial or Lunar-Venus but not Mars-Lunar for example.

We can calibrate the proportions on the circle of types. So we may determine that someone is between Lunar and Venus and observe that they are closer to Lunar. This means they will show mostly Lunar traits with some Venus.

With practice it is feasible to place someone quite accurately on the circle.

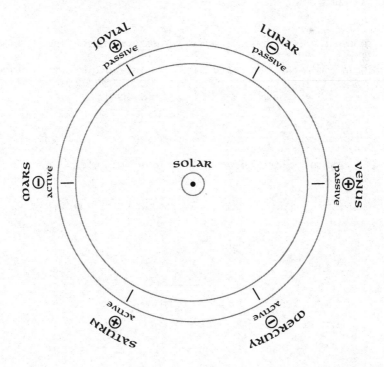

LUNAR-VENUS

A combination of two passive types. The cool withdrawn nature of the Lunar is softened by the warmth and nurturing of Venus. They may combine the stillness of Lunar and the languor of Venus to lead a sedentary lifestyle and can be content to work in an office where they exude a "port in a storm" feeling. They are drawn to serve people and organisations through being steady, reliable and organised; it is easy for active types to overlook their contributions and take them for granted.

This can be a grave error for their steely determination and formidable grasp of procedure is a rock upon which many a high-flyer has foundered. They make fine chess players.

This combination is often found in stable, supportive roles - especially admin positions in health care; NHS offices and the Post Office are home to this type. The 1950s American housewife is a cultural icon.

Kevin Spacey, Norah Jones, Tiger Woods, Lakshmi Mittal, Terry Jones, Humphrey Bogart, Queen Elizabeth II and John Major are examples.

Rabbits, pandas, sheep and the slow-loris are Lunar-Venus animals.

VENUS-MERCURY

The soft languid nature of Venus is toned and speeded up by the hyperactivity of Mercury. The venusian ability to put aside their personality combined with mercurial performing skills produces a seductive, sensual chameleon-like actor. This combination is often highly attractive; Michelangelo's David is a classical example and Angelina Jolie a current one. Flamenco and the Rio de Janeiro carnival are perfect expressions of their glitter and passion. Combining active and passive types can produce intriguing characteristics; a Venus- Mercury may be driven and mercurial at work and venusian and laid-back with their families.

They are also able to choose which side to play off in a given situation. A Venus-Mercury attorney may appear physically slow and inattentive to get someone to drop their guard while their mercurial mind is catching every word and nuance. Catherine Zeta-Jones, Robert de Niro, Jennifer Lopez, Morgan Freeman, Counsellor Troy from Star Trek, Johnny Depp, Carmen Miranda, Al Pacino, Carol Vorderman, Dustin Hoffman and Jessica Rabbit are Venus-Mercurys. Central and South America and most of the Mediterranean are home to this combination.

Chimps, pythons, leopards and dolphins are Venus-Mercurys.

MERCURY-SATURN

Two active types; the quick mind of Mercury allied with Saturn's overview produces a type that does things their way and is a natural leader. Saturns make the rules and Mercurys bend or break the rules. So depending on life influences they can be deeply altruistic or, at the other end of the spectrum, large scale white-collar criminals - literally seeing themselves as "above the law". They can be found leading large charities which operate in lawless areas and need to be creative in rapidly delivering emergency supplies.

With saturnine devotion to a higher cause linked to mercurial drive and expediency they make unique contributions to society. Raul Wallenberg was a Swedish diplomat who issued fake passports and bribed German officials to save an estimated 15,000 Jews from the Holocaust.

A cultural icon is the city gent in a pinstripe suit.

Famous Mercury-Saturns include: Angus Deayton, Grace Jones, John Cleese, Paris Hilton, Barak Obama, Cher, Tony Blair, Elizabeth Hurley, Sacha Baron Cohen, Brooke Shields, Joseph Goebbels, Alistair Campbell, Spike Milligan, Dracula and Osama Bin Laden.

They are often found in dry mountainous regions where survival is challenging and there is often a harsh legal code e. g. Afghanistan and N. E Africa.

Greyhounds, Siamese cats and wolves are Mercury-Saturns.

SATURN-MARS

Two active types: the ascetic ponderous Saturn is turbo-charged by the direct action of Mars to produce a driven, self-reliant pioneer drawn to taking a long hard road to redemption through suffering. Saturn-Mars types are capable of enormous self-sacrifice for the cause of justice and fairness. The cowboy and stoic Victorian explorer are both fuelled by this drive. They make the rules and enforce them; Clint Eastwood plays this combination to perfection. They are found in the US, the Scottish Highlands, Australia and may have a fondness for restrictive paternalistic religious sects. They find it difficult to relax and may lack humour.

Saturn-Mars women are drawn to athletic pursuits, especially tennis and golf.

The cultural icon is the blond-haired blue eyed Aryan Ubermensch of Nazi ideology.

Margaret Thatcher and Arnold Schwarzenegger are Saturn-Mars, also Vikings, the Marlboro man, James Bond, Jodie Foster, Ernest Shackleton, Glenn Close, Livingstone and Stanley, Ann Robinson, Jeremy Paxman, Elizabeth 1st and Julius Caesar – "Veni, vidi, vici".

Golden eagles, pikes, praying mantis, sharks and Alsatian dogs are all Saturn-Mars animals.

MARS-JOVIAL

The bluntness of Mars softened by the tact of Jovial produces an irresistible combination of drive and charm with a strong taste for excess. Mars-Jovial men are often of ruddy complexion, tend to lose their hair at an early age and sweat a lot. Mars –Jovial women are direct and jolly, often happy to drink like "one of the boys" and make outstanding charity fundraisers. They target wealthy potential donors and draw them into the uplifting Jovial orbit. Mars-Jovials make superb generals and politicians; they love to run successful companies and have an open love of money. Due to their reckless bonhomie they bounce back from downturns and many people consider them lucky. Pitfalls come in the form of over indulgence, Jovials want a lot of everything and Mars wants it now, obesity, alcoholism and stress related illnesses are a potential risk. Further on the downside many modern dictators are of this combination; gathering toadies to engage in destructive pursuits e. g. Mussolini, Herman Goering, Stalin, Idi Amin and Slobodan Milosevic.

A cultural icon is the biker and the modern Major General from Gilbert and Sullivan. Janis Joplin and Winston Churchill embody this combination as do Henry the Eighth,Bette Midler, Oliver Reed, Jaime Winstone, Brian Blessed, Sarah Ferguson, Prince Andrew, Herman Goering, John Prescott, Mo Mowlam and Ludwig Van Beethoven.

Bulls, roosters, wild boar and grizzly bears are Mars-Jovial animals.

Mars-Jovials are found in Bavaria and Czech.

JOVIAL-LUNAR

The expansive interests and sociability of the Jovial is tempered by the Lunar ability to focus. This combination invariably has a high IQ; the more Lunar they are, the less likely they are to tell you this and vice versa! They may be socially schizophrenic, out and about for days on end, then at home not answering the phone as they swing from Jovial to Lunar. Jovial-Lunars are often called upon for their expertise and are drawn to homeopathy, science and teaching, especially mathematics. They are often innovators and inventors, enjoying the process of doing things differently. As business consultants they are able to synthesise large amounts of information and produce surprising solutions to challenges. They have a love of logic problems, brain teasers, crosswords and obscure chess openings.

A cultural icon is the female Goth.

They are often solicitors, vicars, comic book dealers, audiophiles and climate change experts. Most successful film directors embody this combination e.g. Peter Brooks, Mike Leigh, Francis Ford Coppola, George Lucas, Pedro Almodovar, Orson Welles, Stanley Kubrick, Ron Howard, Alfred Hitchcock and Ken Burns. Benjamin Franklin, JS Bach, Gordon Brown, Jenny Bond, Kim Il Jong, William Shakespeare, Mr Magoo, Stephen Fry, Michael Gorbachev and Queen Victoria are famous examples.

Gorillas, hippopotami and owls are Jovial-Lunar creatures.

Russia, Korea and Finland are Jovial-Lunar countries.

SOLAR

There is one more element to consider: some people have a third influence. This is represented by the Sun, radiating from the centre of the circle and able to add a vibrational charge which brings a twist to the underlying combination. Any type may have the addition of Solar energy and in varying amounts.

Solars are a positive active type.

Their attention is drawn to bright possibilities and they flutter towards these until exhausted.

Solars can look like fairies; they have large bright eyes set wide apart, delicate cheekbones, fair hair and thin translucent skin.

Their facial expression may be of someone who has just been surprised. They have an androgynous feel and may be fairly asexual though highly attractive. They are skittish and nervous in their movements and may be clumsy. Solars are ungrounded, even unearthly and feel like hummingbirds or hyperactive children in adult bodies. It is as if they retain the charmed aura of childhood where anything seems possible and they have not yet come down to Earth with a bump.

Solars believe in happy endings and will undertake projects no other type would touch. They do not know how to take care of their bodies and lack discrimination – they literally do not know what is good for them.

They may act impulsively and recklessly, believing "the Universe will take care of me".

Other types judge Solars as being ditsy, petulant, childish, attention seeking and as seeing the world through rose-tinted glasses. They see themselves as light, creative, enthusiastic, imaginative, sensitive and artistic. Solars will trust con-men and have difficulty learning from their mistakes as they do not clearly perceive or remember the negative side of life. They love the rarefied atmosphere of the arts and creativity; fashion is a Solar realm and most catwalk models are strongly Solar; usually Solar-Saturns.

Solars see the rest of us as dull, slow, heavy, routine, crass spoilsports. We find them flocking to festivals, crystal shops, art "happenings" and raves. They are open to New Age spiritual ideas and can fall prey to charlatans and "gurus".

Chief feature: Naivety

Solars seem to still live in the magical realm of childhood where anything can happen, the good guys win and the Prince always arrives at the end.
This innocence can remain untouched by experience e.g. Sally Bowles in the film "Cabaret".

As a quality they embody a vibrant, creative energy which inspires and entrances other types. A few moments with a Solar friend are a perfect antidote to cynicism. On the downside they can live in total fantasy, refuse to take responsibility for themselves, be exploited, waste their talents and burn out at an early age.

Solar and rules

Solars do not pay much attention to the rules until they get caught breaking them – they then have a tantrum, forget the potential learning and do it all again.

Solar socially

At a social event they will flock together, gasping and twittering, nibbling sweets and appearing to hover several inches off the ground.

Solar at work

They work well in jobs with creativity and variety and not too much responsibility. They flourish as greeters, florists, fashion designers, cheerleaders, models, children's book authors, ballet dancers and owners of New Age boutiques. Iceland has a high number of Solars; the Wodaabe of Niger is a Solar tribe.

Famous Solars

(In combination with other types)

Solar-Lunar: Meg Ryan, Nancy Reagan, Buster Keaton.

Solar-Venus: Elizabeth Taylor, Clark Gable.

Solar-Venus-Mercury: Elvis Presley, Marilyn Monroe, Betty Boop, Liza Minnelli, Liberace.

Solar-Mercury: Prince, Whitney Houston, Julian Clarey, Joel Grey.

Solar-Mercury-Saturn: Michael Jackson (extremely Solar).

Solar-Saturn: Kate Moss, Laurence Olivier, Barbie, Mozart, Shelley.

Solar-Saturn-Mars: Paul Newman, Princess Diana, McCauley Caulkin, Tilda Swinton.

Solar-Mars: Michelle Pfeiffer, Shirley McClaine, Graham Norton, Goldie Hawn, Shirley Temple, Bette Davis, Madonna.

Solar-Mars-Jovial: Van Morrison.

Solar-Jovial: Benny Hill, Elton John.

Solar animals

Deer, humming birds, skylarks and dragonflies are Solar animals.

RELATIONSHIPS
BETWEEN TYPES

Revisiting the circle of types we have a structure which can bring understanding to the drama of human relationships; at personal, professional and global levels we see how each type reacts to other types in habitual ways. We can come to an understanding of phenomena such as love at first sight, business success or failure, onscreen chemistry and international conflict.

A full exploration requires an entire book so here we have something of an overview. Traveling around the circle and viewing the ways of operating we see three active types – Mercury, Saturn and Mars - and three passive types – Jovial, Lunar and Venus - in sequence. In terms of polarity there are three negative types - Lunar, Mercury and Mars - and three positive types - Venus, Saturn and Jovial - which alternate; it is therefore not possible to embody a combination of two negative or two positive types in one person.

Opposites Attract

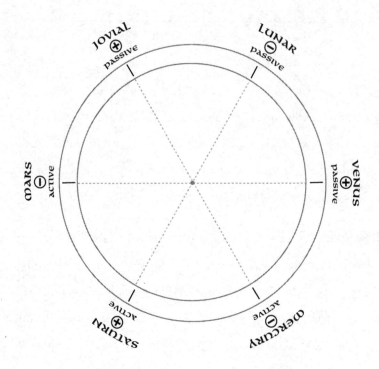

Each type has another one placed directly opposite itself on the circle which is also its opposite in terms of polarity and way of operating:

Saturn, a positive active type, sits opposite the negative passive Lunar.

Mars a negative active type, sits opposite the positive passive Venus.

Jovial, a positive passive type, sits opposite the negative active Mercury.

Each type is electro-magnetically drawn to its opposite. We shall now examine each pair.

SATURN AND LUNAR

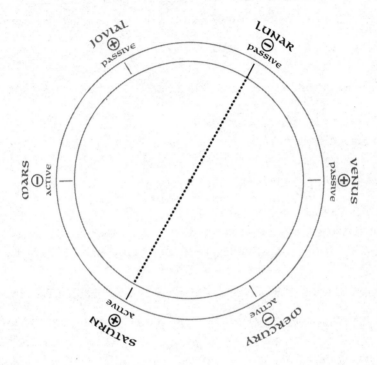

Saturn is seen as the father of the Solar System.

The tall ascetic rule-maker with a chief feature of dominance

Lunar is the child of the Earth.

Quiet and precise, they conform to the rules and have a chief feature
of willfulness.

At a romantic level this can have the flavour of a parent-child dynamic
especially with a Saturn male and Lunar female. Both types appreciate a clean,
well-ordered household with polite offspring and a regular schedule.

As a couple they will enjoy quiet times in each others company, possibly with quirky intellectual pursuits. As hosts they will be more likely to put on a subdued dinner party with classical music in the background than a raucous knees-up.

Their humour will be quite gentle with a weakness for puns. Their children will tend to feel cared for, encouraged and safe rather than showered with love in an exuberant manner.

This will tend to be a stable long lasting relationship as neither type seeks change or drama.

The 1950's middle class suburban American couple epitomizes this dynamic.

Things tend to run like clockwork with the Saturn providing structure and the Lunar supporting and collaborating until the chief features get involved.

Our chief feature is our greatest asset when we use it as a tool for a purpose; the dominance of Saturn creates harmony and safety while the willfulness of Lunar creates stability and clarity.

When our feature is evoked in reaction to another person or to a stressful situation then it becomes our greatest liability.

We are taken over by an energy force which lacks objectivity and wants to win and be right at any cost.

So when Saturn dominance meets Lunar willfulness and they disagree the stage is set for a prolonged struggle. The irresistible force of dominance meets the immovable determination of willfulness. Typically; the Saturn will suggest a course of action, the Lunar will disagree, the Saturn will insist, the Lunar resists, the Saturn seeks to overrule, the Lunar digs in and so on.

When our feature is evoked in interpersonal conflict it evokes the feature in the other person.

Escalation follows unless one party becomes aware of their own inner dynamic, takes a breath and returns to a place of compassion. Very often at this point the feature of the other person will feel cheated of the chance to fight and try twice as hard to re-evoke the other feature.

The phrase "pushing someone's buttons" is often a euphemism for evoking their chief feature.

To the outside observer it seems that the overbearing Saturn is the favourite to win this fight. We tend to overlook the power of passivity, very often sheer willful refusal to budge or engage wears down the opponent. Lunars also have a love of chess and strategy and it may well be that they lose the battle and go on to win the war.

Globally we see this dynamic in post war India. For 200 years the Saturn institute of the British Empire had dominated largely Lunar India. The British imposed their language, education system, customs, religion and business practices on a culture that was 5000 years old; all in the name of progress. Mahatma Gandhi, who was close to being a pure Lunar type, decided to resist using Satyagraha – non-violent direct action. He simply said "No" to the rules and was willing to be beaten and imprisoned without ever striking back.

This struck a deep chord in the psyche of India and after many attempts to reassert dominance the British were astute enough to withdraw. There is archival footage of the British flag coming down while the Indian flag is raised. Lord Louis Mountbatten, six feet five inches of Saturn stiff upper lip salutes stiffly while at his side Gandhi, five feet three inches looks directly at the camera with a twinkle of mischief in his eye. Passivity is a powerful force.

In the workplace we see Lunars in administrative positions who may wield immense power simply by regulating the speed with which procedures take place. When Saturns and Lunars work harmoniously then an enterprise is like a well oiled machine e.g. a Swiss bank, operating theatre or finance department. When dominance and willfulness are in conflict then the whole thing mysteriously grinds to a halt until equilibrium is restored – often with a private abject apology offered by a Saturn to a Lunar! Suddenly things start to flow again.

Famous examples of Saturn-Lunar couples include: Prince Philip and Queen Elizabeth 2nd. Heather Mills and Paul McCartney (willfulness won that courtroom battle!), Margot and Jerry from the TV show *The Good Life*, Ron and Nancy "just say no" Reagan, Julian Sands and Helena Bonham Carter in the film *Room With a View*, Gwyneth Paltrow and Chris Martin.

For a comedic take; the "End of the World" skit from *The Secret Policeman's Ball* is an exquisite play of dominance and willfulness between Peter Cook and Rowan Atkinson.

As material for a superb film *Harold and Maude* takes this dynamic to creative extremes.

MARS AND VENUS

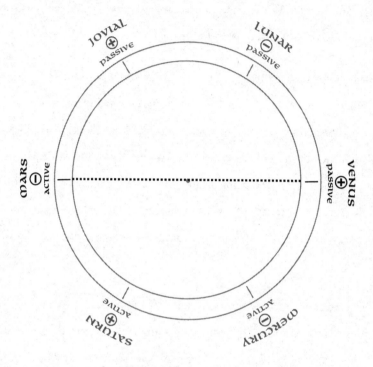

Mars is the warrior of the Solar System.

Compact and driven, they have a chief feature of destruction.

Venus is the Mother of the Solar System.

Soft and languorous, they have a chief feature of non-existence.

In mythology Mars and Venus were lovers and depicted in numerous classical works of art

Typically they are shown post-coital with Mars asleep and Venus alert and cheerful symbolizing that Love conquers War.

In the painting *Venus and Mars* by Sandro Botticelli; Mars snores obliviously while satyrs play with his lance, showing that he has been disarmed. One cherub even blows a trumpet in his ear to demonstrate that Mars is out for the count. Venus looks quite content.

In the field of romance this is a relationship fueled by passion. The robust, highly adrenalised Mars is strongly drawn to the sensual softness of Venus and Venus is enlivened by the charge of Mars' energy. The relationship will not be dull with Venus trying to keep up with the pace of Mars life while Mars is torn between the habit of forging ahead alone and the temptation to sink blissfully into the sanctuary of the Venus embrace. Venus is content to wait while Mars battles the world; knowing that her inert seductive power will pull him back.

This can be a tremendously successful relationship; especially when an ambitious Mars male enters the corporate arena with a Venus partner supporting him. He is able to fully engage in the workplace and return home to feel nurtured and recharged. Venus is able to take pride in the success of Mars without having to struggle on the front line. At its best this relationship is passionate, straightforward, and exciting.

There is a juicy, life-affirming feeling to be experienced in their company. The children have the advantage of the safety and support of Venus and the encouragement from Mars to step out into the world and grab hold of life. This dynamic can be just as powerful if the genders are reversed although Western culture has idealized the Mars male doer and Venus female carer which further reinforces the tendencies.

When this relationship is dysfunctional we find the Venus partner becomes the outlet for the pent up frustrations of Mars. With the addition of alcohol it is easy for this to tip into physical violence; the feature of destruction meets non-existence. When increasing destruction is met by increasing non-existence the frustration builds to dangerous levels as Mars is not getting the direct confrontation it seeks and Venus is not finding the security it hopes to gain by surrendering. At any domestic violence shelter this will be verbalized in phrases such as: "I should have had the dinner ready on time", "He takes such good care of the kids", "He's lovely when he doesn't drink" and "It was my own fault for nagging him". The Venus ability to put oneself aside in service of another has become pathological and tipped into self blaming and a willingness to endure abuse. It can be quite a challenge to convince a Venus type that they deserve better.

It is difficult for other types to comprehend the strength of attraction between these two so we shall use an historical example.

HMS Bounty sailed to Tahiti in 1789 to make astrological observations. Captain William Bligh was an outstanding navigator and a Lunar type. It is reasonable to assume that the crew of an armed Royal Navy vessel was composed almost exclusively of Mars men. Lacking any sense of irony they landed at Venus Point. Once in Tahiti the crew met and fraternized with the local Venus women for several months. Once his highly precise observations of the transit of the planet Venus were complete, Bligh ordered the crew to sail back to England. This presented the crew with a difficult dilemma; they wanted to stay with the Tahitian women and vice versa, but to disobey an order meant mutiny. The penalty for mutiny was to be hunted down relentlessly by the most powerful navy in the world and tortured to death. The attraction was so strong that the crew chose to send Captain Bligh and some of his officers off to what seemed like certain death in a small boat and to make off with

the Bounty.

Mars types will enforce the rules when they believe they are fair but will take drastic action in rebelling against unfair rules. In this case they chose to risk lingering death rather than leave the Venus women of Tahiti. Bligh survived one of the most extraordinary journeys a boat had ever undertaken and the rest is history.

Mars and Venus can also make really solid best friends – they just "click".

In the workplace it is common to see a Mars salesman make a beeline for a Venus colleague to share war stories and receive a pat on the back and sympathetic ear before charging back to the front line refreshed.

Famous examples of Mars-Venus couples include: Chris Evans and Billie Piper, Wayne and Colleen Rooney, Sharon and Ozzie Osbourne, Lord Nelson "Never mind tactics-go straight at them! " and Lady Hamilton, Melanie Griffiths and Antonio Banderas and Emperor Hadrian and Antonius.

For a portrayal of the dark side of this relationship see Richard Burton and Elizabeth Taylor in *Who's Afraid of Virginia Woolf*

To appreciate the onscreen chemistry this relationship creates regardless of gender or sexual orientation see Heath Ledger and Jake Gylenhaal in *Brokeback Mountain*

JOVIAL AND MERCURY

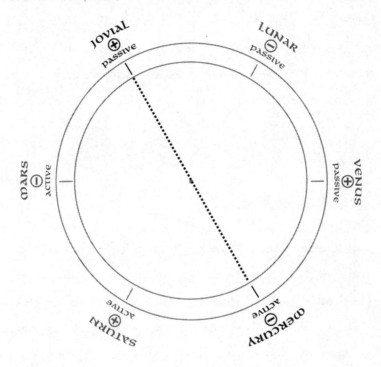

Jupiter is the regal grandparent of the Solar System.

Radiant and generous with a chief feature of vanity.

Mercury is the mischievous grandchild.

Quick-witted and charming with a chief feature of power.

In romance and friendship this relationship has the feel of a jovial monarch engaging with a mercurial court jester. Jovials have an expansive mind which relishes following the twists and turns of the ever shifting Mercury.

Their relationship has strong elements of play, wit and drama. Jovials love to throw lavish parties where Mercurys show up and entertain. The jester plays a sacred historical role; the monarch is seen as akin to a God on Earth and beyond reproach, so only the jester is allowed to make fun of the monarch and at great personal risk. The jester must maintain a delicate balance by making light of the shortcomings of the monarch using humour. This way the monarch gets to indirectly hear the truth of how he is perceived by his subjects. The jester walks a tightrope between either being too obsequious or offending the monarch. To find the balance brings great reward but to offend the monarch results in being beheaded.

They share a love of the arts especially opera and classical music and it is typically the Jovial that generates the income to spend on these pursuits. If their features of power and vanity become predominant this couple can tend to crimes of excess and deception; Conrad Black and Barbara Amiel are prime examples of a Jovial urged to ever greater consumption in league with the creative spending talents of Mercury.

In a relationship there is constant movement and interaction and it is likely both parties will feel they have a hard time getting a word in edgeways; Jovials love to talk, especially about themselves and Mercurys often talk rapidly and incessantly. When in harmony they create a crackling atmosphere of bright possibilities and interpersonal connections. They delight in each other's company, the Mercury able to flatter and entrance the Jovial who provides an appreciative and warm audience. When their features come into conflict the Mercury will be merciless in teasing the Jovial and willing to push on all the weakest spots, despising the Jovial for needing their positive feedback.

The Jovial, sensitive underneath the bluster will feel wounded and taken for granted, even exploited. As a passive type they will tend to withdraw and essentially banish the Mercury from the Royal circle until they come to heel.

Having withdrawn, a Jovial is prone to sulk and revisit the wounds inflicted by the Mercury.

The Jovial King George IV was crushed when out with a companion he met his former friend the Mercury Beau Brummel who blatantly ignored the King and said to his companion, "Who's your fat friend?".

This impasse is typically broken when each has missed the company of the other and the Mercury will make peace by complimenting the Jovial, never by apologizing. It is extremely rare for either of these types to apologise. The Mercury sees an apology as losing face and a Jovial sees it as beneath their dignity.

In a romantic relationship it can happen that the Mercury seduces someone else, the Jovial is mortally offended by this and totally erases the Mercury from their life; even to the extent of forbidding mutual friends to mention them. Mercury can never resist such a huge challenge and never take "No" for an answer; so will begin a relentless campaign of flattery.

The more determined Jovial's resistance, the thicker the flattery until the Jovial crumbles. There is a tearful reunion; promises to never re-offend are issued and everyone celebrates.

This process can be repeated many times; see Bill and Hilary Clinton.

In the workplace it is common to see a Jovial mentor encouraging a Mercury protégée. It is not uncommon to see the Jovial feeling like a rung on a ladder at some future point.

This pairing is very often seen in the comedic double-act: *Laurel and Hardy*, *The Fast Show*, *The Two Ronnies*, *Morecambe and Wise*, Johnny Carson and Ed McMann, *French and Saunders*, Little and Large, Ant and Dec, *Little Britain*, Eric Sykes and Hattie Jacques, Blair and Prescott, Bird and Fortune – the list goes on.

Famous couples include Elton John and Furness, Louis XVI and Marie Antoinette, Ferdinand and Imelda Marcos, Toad and Ratty from Wind in the Willows, Richard and Judy, Dick Dastardly and Muttley and the warthog and the meerkat from *The Lion King*.

Other Relationships

Revisiting the circle as a template, we can examine two triads of polarity:

Positive polarity: Jovial, Saturn and Venus. The positive types tend to be more tolerant of each other.

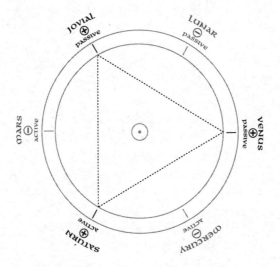

Negative polarity: Mars, Lunar and Mercury. The negative types tend to be less tolerant of each other.

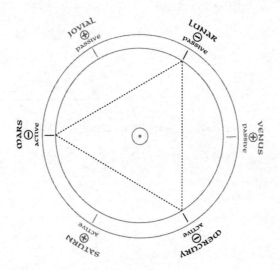

Positive Triad
JOVIALS AND VENUS

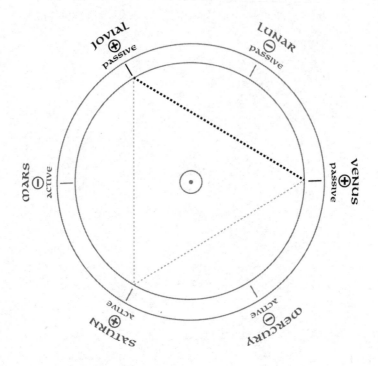

These two can be difficult to tell apart, both tend to be large and fond of people. They are both positive and passive. One distinguishing factor is that Venus types tend to live through other people whereas Jovials gather satellites as a positive reflection of themselves.

They have different agendas and ways of operating and seldom come into conflict, especially as both are passive. If they don't get along they will simply drift away from each other.

Positive Triad
SATURNS AND JOVIALS

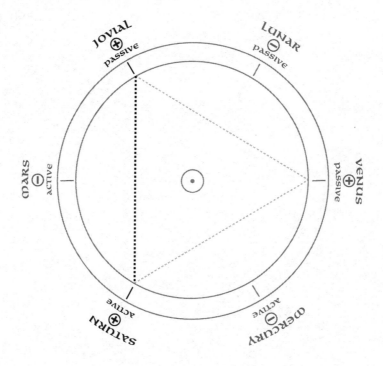

They differ in physical stature and in that Jovials are passive while Saturns are active. Saturns often see Jovials as immodest and unfocussed while Jovials view Saturns as stiff and grey. Each type is able to appreciate the strengths of the other and they can form effective business partnerships where Saturn provides structure and direction and the Jovial brings people into the project.

Their likeliest area of conflict is in mentoring where they can compete for a protégée; the Saturn wishing to play the paternal coaching role and the Jovial wanting to play the wise grandparent. The potential protégée can feel like a wishbone.

Positive Triad

SATURNS AND VENUS

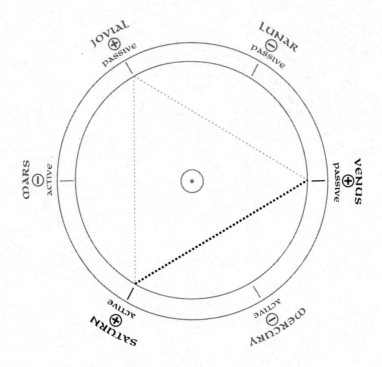

These two tend to operate in different realms and in different ways. They rarely have conflict due largely to the non-existence of Venus. Saturns can have a slightly sniffy disapproval of Venuses, seeing them as unmotivated and adrift while Venuses get niggled by the feeling of being looked down upon. They tend to simply avoid each other rather than argue, sometimes with a touch of sighing and eye-rolling from the Saturn who may say, "Well I tried but they just don't seem to want to make the effort".

Negative Triad
LUNAR AND MERCURY

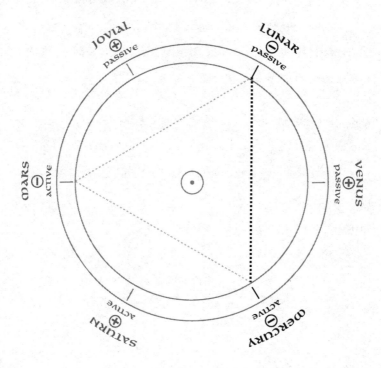

Often playing quite different roles in life, Lunars are passive and usually withdrawn while Mercurys are active and highly engaged with others.

Their respective features provide rich material for conflict, Lunars are willful and keep the rules; once a Lunar has said No they will stick with it. Mercurys have a chief feature of power and bend or break the rules; they never take "No for an answer" so will turn on their persuasive talents to get what they want.

Both types are equally motivated to never lose face; so Lunars avoid losing their cool and Mercurys avoid being thwarted, especially in public.

A bank is a good arena in which to observe a Mercury customer attempting to coerce a Lunar clerk into "relaxing the guidelines just this once". On a larger scale, within a company, we see the sales department asking for more advertising spend and getting shot down by the finance department. Being passive, a Lunar will not seek conflict with a Mercury but when pushed and manipulated they make a formidable opponent.

Japan and China have played out this drama. Most Mercurys are astute enough to learn this lesson the first time around and content themselves with teasing the Lunar and giving the occasional back-handed compliment. In collaboration, Mercurys explore and exploit new territories while Lunars create order so nothing falls through the cracks.

Negative Triad
LUNAR AND MARS

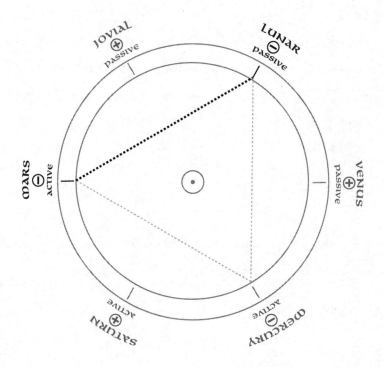

They usually play different roles in life; the active Mars is on the front line pushing through barriers, the passive Lunars more often in the background preserving the status quo.

Each type has respect for the different flavours of self reliance of the other. Lunars are able to flourish with limited space and resources while Mars endure and even relish discomfort. They can make firm friends if they give each other space, both valuing loyalty and honesty.

Their different speeds of operation create frustration; Mars wants to go from A to B immediately while Lunars want all the forms filled in before they sign the cheque.

Mars hate detail as much as Lunars love it. In a company this is the flashpoint between a Lunar finance and admin department and a Mars operations department. Ops wants to get it done on time, finance is waiting for the purchase order.

In conflict Mars will rage and push while a Lunar will refuse to fight and continually refer back to the rules. The fight will typically end when the Mars goes away; if they do succeed in overpowering the Lunar the Mars will forget about it once they have eventually calmed down. The Lunar will not forget about it, a rematch will follow in good time, the Lunar will win.

Negative Triad

MARS AND MERCURY

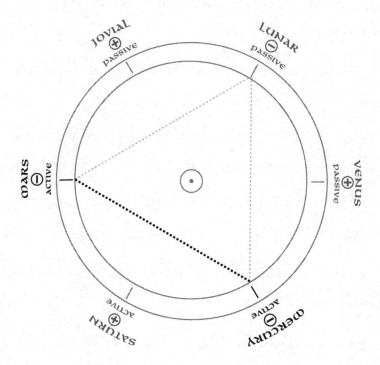

This dynamic can provide enough material for an entire book; it has been a rich seam of drama throughout human history and will continue to provide material, at great human cost, for as long we remain unconscious of the hidden forces at work.

Mars is a negative active type; direct and blunt, they enforce the rules and thrive on confrontation.

Mercury is also negative and active but in totally different and often antagonistic ways.

Mercurys are indirect, expedient, bend or break the rules and hate being pinned down.

These two can get along, even enjoy each other's company and humour, but when their features are evoked it gets unpleasant and often escalates.

Both types are of negative polarity so they notice and can fixate on the worst in each other.

Both types are active, so unlike passive types they cannot leave each other alone, they are compelled to act.

Mars is the archetypal policeman, protecting the vulnerable from exploitation and bullying.

They have a literal view of right and wrong, this helps them find solid ground on which to stand firm and act decisively on the side of the good guys.
This is not to say there are not Mars types who commit crime, if they do it will usually be in a direct way, often using violence and intimidation.

A good casting director will have a Mars type playing a crusading policeman as this will instinctively feel right to the audience eg Nick Nolte, Brian Dennehy, David Caruso, John Thaw, Denis Waterman and Helen Mirren.

Mercurys will almost inevitably be cast as the villain, to the point where in silent films it is a cliché to see the shifting eyes, black moustache and slinking gestures of the bad guy; these are mercurial characteristics exaggerated to broadcast their deviousness.

The rapid mind and creative thinking, coupled with their impatience lead Mercurys into grey areas around the rules; they see the rules as something to be tested and probed.

They make accomplished stage hypnotists and magicians and devote time to the study of human suggestibility and gullibility e. g. David Blaine, Derren Brown and David Copperfield. This is not to say that Mercurys inherently lean towards criminality or that the vast majority are not scrupulously honest and law abiding; it means that their innate talents can lend themselves to a certain flexibility in this realm. If a Mercury does cross the line into criminal activity it will often be around fraud, deception, boiler room sales and pyramid schemes rather than violent crime; Del Boy Trotter being an endearing example.

So the stage is set for an age old struggle between two impatient, active, highly energised types who react to each other like the same poles of two magnets; there is repulsion and the potential for huge conflict – an archetypal, mythological struggle which plays out daily in offices, families and in the global arena.

Mars see Mercurys as devious, slippery, manipulative and unscrupulous; they sense that Mercurys are up to something bad; they want to catch them red handed, extract a confession then see them punished severely and publicly.

Mercurys see Mars as bull-headed, literal, plodding and blinkered; they cannot resist teasing and tricking them and are amazed and delighted that Mars repeatedly falls for their schemes.

This of course enrages Mars further and increases their determination to grab and batter Mercury. Mercurys are fond of posturing and implied threat but have very little taste for physical violence, preferring a war of words that can tie their opponent in knots.

Spain is a Mercury country which has made a ritual of this struggle, they take a Mars bull, stick spikes in it and torment it until it is in a murderous rage; at his point a small Mercury matador steps out in his finest outfit and proceeds to trick the bull into charging at his cape while standing within inches of the deadly horns.
As Spain is a Mercury nation the Mars bull usually loses.

In Mars Britain a different ritual is enacted, the fox hunt; small Mercury creature chased relentlessly by people on horses dressed in red.
They like the fox to lose or at least win fairly.

Once the features of power and destruction are evoked in opposition it is difficult for either party to let go of the urge to triumph and each has a totally different view of victory and resolution. It is instructive to see warfare in this context, by taking a global view we can apply the Hermetic principle and gain insight into the nature of this dynamic at a personal level.

North-western Europe is a largely Saturn-Mars culture which we see idealised in Norse mythology, mediaeval knighthood and the Aryan ideal. The method of war is one that is brutal and direct yet has notions of fair play; in mediaeval times the opposing forces would meet at an arranged time and place, start promptly, battle all day and there would be a clear winner and loser.
The winner would receive territory and ransom money and both sides would go home until the next time. It was almost like a football match but with more casualties.

Their expectation was that all wars were fought in that manner. When the first Crusade was launched in 1096 to take Jerusalem back from the Muslim armies the crusaders were to encounter a different way of waging war. There were no set piece battles, troupes of horsemen would attack at the weakest points, kill a few people and make off with booty.

The enemy would be seen, battle lines were formed and the enemy would then ride off and reappear behind them. This is the Mercury way of war, feints, concealment, betrayal, sneak attacks and rapid retreats; it is effective at wearing down and frustrating the enemy without incurring high casualties.

The current situation in Iraq and Afghanistan has been compared by George W. Bush to a modern crusade and there are many parallels. Christianity is a Saturn-Mars religion and Islam a Mercury one – the faith of the word.
The "Worlds Policeman" has shown up for a fight and is not sure who or where the enemy is. Osama Bin Laden is out there somewhere taunting the West with videos. Saddam Hussein was found hiding in a hole in the ground.

Mercury will not stand in front of the bull – why would they?

Mars continues to charge at thin air – how can they stop?

The Iraq situation has also been compared to Vietnam, an unseen enemy using snipers and booby traps, hiding amongst civilians. This dynamic plays out repeatedly and has done throughout history. During the Holocaust the Mars fury of Germany was unleashed upon the Mercury races of Europe; Jews, Slavs and Gypsies and the goal was nothing short of total annihilation. The Nazis were so fixated on the Final Solution that they diverted transport and manpower from the front line to maintain the giant killing machine.

This is a visceral, primal hatred which periodically erupts. When a Mars nation is under stress it will attack and seek to obliterate Mercury. When Mercury Japan attacked Pearl Harbour the unfairness spurred the United States into a massive response in World War Two.

When good old Saturn-Mars Margaret Thatcher was on the ropes it was time to beat up Mercury Argentina over the Falklands.

Shakespeare gave us Othello, the warrior Moor tricked into destructive rage by the innuendo of his trusted lieutenant Iago. Mercury can be very adept at turning one against oneself.

Hollywood has made a film purely devoted to this drama; *Terminator 2 Judgement Day* pits Saturn-Mars Arnold Shwartzeneggar the old style solid metal terminator against Mercury Robert Patrick as the shiny new T1000 made of liquid metal i. e. mercury which can change into any form.
Arnie must protect the young boy from the T1000 sent to kill him.

Arnie plays it straight and tough while the T1000 plays all kinds of tricks and cannot be destroyed by guns or explosions. I won't spoil the ending.

Mercurys never give up, even when they are beaten, Dracula is a Mercury and has to be killed in very specific ways or he returns when you least expect him. Peter Mandelson has a similar political history. This drives Mars crazy, they want to catch Mercury in the act so they will see the error of their ways and never do it again. Mars believes in redemption through suffering; we experience the pain of seeing that we have sinned, acknowledge this and promise never to be bad again. For this reason they can be drawn to 'Born Again' Christianity.

Mercury sees the sin is in being caught rather than the transgression and their focus is more on learning to avoid recapture than on not re-offending.
If they need to promise not to do it again in order to be released then they will promise - with one eye on a get-out clause.

The film *One Flew over the Cuckoo's Nest* has the Mercury Jack Nicholson battling the Mars Louis Fletcher as Nurse Ratched. The heart of the film is the gradual escalation of the conflict until we see the raw features in all out war. One effect of Jack Nicholson's Mercury inspired talent is to awaken the Native American played by Will Sampson from extreme Venusian non-existence.

The recent film *Happy Go Lucky* has a remarkable Mars-Mercury explosion at its core. Bette Davies and Joan Crawford inhabited these roles onstage and off stage.

In his book *Cities of the Plain* Cormac McCarthy writes an account of a knife fight between an American cowboy and a Mexican pimp which perfectly reflects Mars and Mercury.

In the world of nature there are only two species other than humans which will attack and kill each other out of mutual hatred; this is the Mars lion and Mercury hyena.

Both species live in packs in close proximity and lead different lives; lions hunt, eat and sleep while hyenas scavenge and are constantly on the move looking for opportunities. A full grown male lion is strong and fast enough to kill a hyena and a large enough pack of hyenas can overwhelm and kill a weak lion. So they live in a macabre balance. These are the only animals that mark their territory to exclude another species; all other animals mark territory to exclude other members of the same species from their hunting ground; lions and hyenas will draw a line that the other pack crosses at their peril.

This is shown in a spellbinding National Geographic video titled *Eternal Enemies*.

The antidote to this unconscious play of features is awareness; if we are aware of types it is possible to take a half-step back and see the feature attempting to take over one's body.

We then have a moment of choice – to react or to respond. If we have this battle of features between friends or acquaintances in our life the best move is to encourage them to take time and space to find perspective and see if they can let go of winning and being right.

The world would be a far duller place without the thrilling energetic input of Mars and Mercury and a far more peaceful place with a little more compassion and understanding between them.

a caveat

Dear reader, having read this far you may wish to use this knowledge in your daily life.

The purpose of this book is to deepen compassion for yourself and others through increased understanding.

Please begin by applying the Socratic injunction "Know Thyself".

Observe yourself as if you are an interesting stranger and avoid judging what you see. This is not a guide for "self improvement" this is the owner's manual for your vehicle.

Get to know it and an interesting process unfolds: the "strengths" that your ego had claimed as uniquely yours are seen simply as characteristics of your type; as are the "weaknesses" that you may have been ashamed of .

We can come to take ourselves less personally and less seriously.

"Out on the edge of town
Beyond the place of Right and Wrong
There is a field
Let us meet there"
– Rumi

If you try to explain this system to the people close to you they will think you are mad; for it is not rational, logical or easy to explain.

Give yourself some time to understand and verify the system before you tell others – seven years is reasonable preparation.

If you tell other people their type and how to improve they may well become angry and feel that you are labeling and judging them.

No type is better or worse than any other.

Observe people at work; when you walk into a library or bank see how many Lunars work there; challenge yourself and see if you can find a policeman who is not a Mars.

Get a feel for each type; gradually you build a sense of each one.

Focus on the inherent qualities of each type; see what you appreciate in friends and family.

Notice how each type serves others in unique ways.

The cool persistence, un-shakable poise, clarity, quirky wit and discipline of Lunar.

The support, unconditional acceptance, healing aura, caring and nurturing of Venus.

The wit, sparkle, mischief, restless enquiring mind and playful delight of Mercury.

The benign fatherly influence, guidance, fairness and selfless devotion of Saturn.

The courage, strength, protectiveness, loyalty, honesty and commitment of Mars.

The warmth, generosity, tact, radiance, grandeur, dignity and booming laugh of Jovial.

The openness, delight, creativity, breathless enthusiasm and ethereal innocence of Solar.

Notice how much influence your own type has in every arena of your life and how difficult it is to act otherwise.

Feel free to laugh out loud when you see your feature in action.

It becomes so much easier to accept yourself and others and *vive la différence*!

Most importantly-this system simply describes your physical vehicle; within this marvelous vehicle is a unique spark of Existence traveling through life on Earth.

Enjoy the ride!

ABOUT THE AUTHOR

John Cremer is a speaker, trainer and improviser. He has spent over 20 years studying the principles behind *Reading People* and refining his methods by working with a huge range of clients.

Initially intrigued with the practical applications, he has since researched the fascinating historical roots of this unique system. John finds these new connections and deeper insights enrich his personal and professional life every day.

His journey in personal development began in Phoenix Arizona in 1985 with Omega Vector, an organisation that offered intensive awareness trainings. John worked as a trainer in the organisation and went on to work with groups devoted to exploring human potential. He joined the Oxymorons Improvisation Troupe, directing and performing in hundreds of shows under the guidance of the legendary Louis Anthony Russo. John was invited to perform with Essential Theatre Playback Company, which gave totally improvised plays based on stories from audience members.

Returning to the UK in 2001 John founded the Maydays award-winning improvisation troupe and performs with them regularly. The Maydays give public shows of hilarious *Whose Line is it Anyway?* style improvisation and are renowned for their totally improvised musicals. They create bespoke shows and trainings for companies and organisations. Every troupe member gets to know their own type and that of their colleagues as a way of heightening their performance skill level. They work with a diverse range of clients including Legal and General, the British Council, Friends of the Earth and won Best Comedy Show Brighton Festival Fringe 2007.

www.themaydays.co.uk

"The Maydays' performance was the highlight of our 2008 clergy conference - hilarious, clever and pitched perfectly for the audience. They enthralled us by turning our suggestions and comments into comic turns and songs. The laughter never stopped and it was all totally appropriate - slightly cheeky but never offensive. They got the audience on their side from the start, and the mood of happiness and delight lingered long after they'd left the stage."
– The Rt Revd Graham James, Bishop of Norwich

John is a fellow of the Professional Speakers Association and gives keynote talks and improvisation skills training to companies and organisations such as: T-Mobile, Deloitte, Microsoft, Airbus, Vistage and was awarded Star Speaker 2007 by the Academy for Chief Executives.

When he is not speaking, training, writing, researching or performing he can often be spotted, rod in hand, stalking the elusive sea trout and bass from Brighton beach.

John is author of the book "IMPROV Enjoy life and success with the Power of Yes"

This material is best-learned first-hand from an experienced practitioner.
John Cremer offers the following to companies and organisations:

READING PEOPLE WORKSHOPS

1. A half-day Reading People Workshop
for a maximum of twelve participants

Programme

The system is revealed in a clear and precise manner, each type is explored in detail using examples from history, members' own lives and contemporary culture. We look at the typical occupations for each type and also their worst possible jobs. The group creates an ideal company using the system and also finds the precise recipe for business failure - which can be just as useful to know. The relationships and misunderstandings that arise naturally between types are addressed and solutions are explored. Each participant has the option to discover their own type and look at the implications this has in their personal and professional life. Time and willingness permitting, we use role-play and improvisation to experience the nature of one's type.

There is a strong thread of humour running through the session, as nothing is funnier than human nature.

Outcomes

Members come away with practical knowledge of the system and the potential applications. The number of "Ahas" can be extraordinary; the information is fascinating, for some it is life changing. This system can help put into concrete terms insights we have into others but do not have a context for. On a personal level, members come to greater acceptance of themselves and other people. Once we see the influence one's type has it becomes easy to let go of expecting others to be different.

Professionally the amount of money and energy saved when we find the right type for the job is enormous.

A concise, purpose written workbook that reinforces the learning is available.

2. A full day Reading People Masterclass

This goes deeper into the personal learning and applications. There is time for a question and answer session that facilitates hands-on applications of the system using real life situations.

3. A keynote talk on Reading People

Lively and humorous yet has a profound effect when delegates reflect upon the material. Time permitting we use volunteers from the audience as examples of types. Visual aids and short movie clips enrich the learning process.

4. Breakout sessions on Reading People for conferences

This adds a completely different dimension to an event, learning can be put into practice immediately and can be a revelation in large groups.

5. Bespoke Reading People Training

To raise the awareness level of a team, explore habitual dynamics and unlock hidden potential. These are especially powerful when applied for a specific purpose or in a retreat setting. Can be a one-off, a series or ongoing.

"The management team had a great time learning this unique high impact material. They found it eye opening, as well as highly practical in the workplace. We came away with a better understanding of ourselves, our clients and each other. Many in the group found insight into their personal relationships and felt they could now understand their partners and children better."
– Chris Davis, CEO Dunlop Systems & Components Limited

"Content & Presentation: - 10/10. Fantastic, captivating, enthralling, brilliant, would like to do a full day session." – Paul Scanlon, Chairman CDP Print Management

"Thank you for your masterclass performance yesterday. Reading People was a resounding success. Your command of the subject, your inspirational style backed up by your astonishing verbal dexterity made for one of the greatest Academy days I have experienced. One member scored you straight tens, and said it was "the most enjoyable morning that he has had since joining the Academy".
– Joe Adams, Chairman Group 11 Academy for Chief Executives

"This has been without doubt the most worthwhile personnel management and HR/ personal/ professional development course that I have ever attended. John's presentation style is truly inspiring, he engages with participants at a remarkable level. I'm recommending this course to everyone!"
– John Nicholls, MD London Calling Arts

IMPROVISATION WORKSHOPS

John Cremer is founder of the Maydays improvisation troupe www.themaydays.co.uk and also offers training and talks entitled *The Fine Art of Improvisation*.

This can be offered in the following formats: -

Breakout sessions at a conference from 45-90 minutes. These are highly interactive, fast-paced and utterly hilarious. Delegates also take away potent tools to implement during and after the event.

Half-day training. These sessions are hands-on, enthralling, utterly unique, quite silly and deeply profound in the after effects. These are in high demand for retreats as they create bonding in new groups and transform dynamics in established groups.

Keynote talk with or without bringing audience volunteers onstage for "on the spot" improvisation skills training. These get audiences involved, laughing a lot and thinking along very different lines.

Bespoke improvised comedy shows for any event. This highly interactive presentation gives participants an experience of using techniques which:

- Enhance personal effectiveness and confidence under pressure.

- Access "out of the box" innovative thinking and problem solving.

- Reduce stress levels and misunderstanding by promoting positive interpersonal communication.

- Quickly and deeply bond and inspire a team.

- Create an enjoyable and productive work environment which increases staff retention.

Approach

An experiential process in which simple tools are learned and applied in a series of increasingly challenging exercises. There is laughter galore as participants are taken progressively outside of their comfort zone in a supportive, exciting atmosphere.

The skills acquired are embodied and not just theorised.

The personal and professional benefits and challenges are explored as they arise.

One side benefit is that the group as a whole becomes more bonded, open and supportive – members are very often surprised by the hidden talent of people they have known for years!

Benefits

Members take away simple yet highly effective tools that enable instant access to higher levels of confidence and creative thinking. They learn techniques of brainstorming and problem solving which engage the latent potential of teams.

The group itself often shifts out of habitual dynamics, becoming flexible and more able to address uncomfortable subjects. Often the quiet members speak up more and the noisy ones listen better!

Participants report improved communications with staff and a positive impact on morale and engagement.

Recent clients include: Friends of the Earth, the British Council, Legal and General and Norfolk Diocese Ecclesiastical Conference.

"The techniques of improvisation go straight to the heart of what it takes to be an effective leader. CEO's need to make instant judgements and decisions, often without preparation and then commit to seeing them through. This workshop provides a safe environment where CEO's can practice these skills without fear of failure or ridicule and can even learn to laugh at their mistakes". – Simon Lester: CEO, Lester Hotels Group